THE BLESSING CANDLES

58 Simple Mealtime Prayer-Celebrations

GAYNELL BORDES CRONIN

JACK RATHSCHMIDT, O.F.M. CAP.

ST. ANTHONY MESSENGER PRESS

Cincinnati, Ohio

Excerpt from a passage by Molly Fumia from *Prayers for Healing* edited by Maggie Oman, copyright ©1997 by Maggie Oman, is reprinted by permission of Conari Press.

Excerpt from *Love Is a Stranger,* by Jalal Al-Din Rumi, copyright ©1993 by Jalal Al-Din Rumi, is reprinted by permission of Shambhala Publications.

Excerpt from "Choruses from 'The Rock,'" from T.S. Eliot's *Collected Poems 1909-1962,* copyright ©1936 by Harcourt, Inc., copyright ©1963 by T.S. Eliot, is reprinted by permission of Harcourt Brace.

Excerpt from Jessica Powers' *Selected Poetry,* copyright ©1989, by Jessica Powers is reprinted by permission of the Institute for Carmelite Studies.

Excerpts from *Life Prayers: From Around the World, 365 Prayers, Blessings, and Affirmations to Celebrate the Human Journey,* edited by Elizabeth J. Roberts and Elias Amidon, copyright ©1996 by Elizabeth J. Roberts and Elias Amidon, are reprinted by permission of HarperSanFrancisco.

Excerpt from *Meditations With Meister Eckhart,* trans. Matthew Fox, copyright ©1983, by Matthew Fox, is reprinted by permission of Bear and Co.

Unless otherwise noted, Scripture citations are taken from the *New Revised Standard Version Bible,* copyright © 1998 by the Division of Christian Education of the National Council of Churches of Christ in the U.S.A. Used by permission. All rights reserved.

Cover and interior illustrations by Mary Newell DePalma
Cover and book design by Constance Wolfer

ISBN 0-86716-379-8

Copyright © 2000, Gaynell Bordes Cronin and Jack Rathschmidt, O.F.M. Cap.
All rights reserved.

Published by St. Anthony Messenger Press
www.AmericanCatholic.org
Printed in the U.S.A.

For children and families of the twenty-first century:

May we continue to believe
that it is our faith heritage, right, joy and privilege
to pray at home.

*C*ontents

Blessings for Special Occasions

Blessings for the Year

Acknowledgments

For all, especially our families and the children in them, who recognize and express ritually the nearness of God in their everyday life, day after day, year after year. Thank you. Thank you. You are the light of the blessing candles.

*I*ntroduction

When we went to Nanan's, my Great-aunt Germaine's home, we always gathered around her great oak table for dinner. Covered with a handmade cloth—a family heirloom made by her grandmother and brought to New Orleans from her home in Alsace Lorraine—the oak table also held two candles with flowers placed between them. That table was magical! Almost as soon as the candles were kindled, the stories, which seemed to go on forever, began. My child's eyes and heart knew that I was safe and belonged to family whenever we gathered around that table. Nanan's simple, two-candle ritual not only rooted me in my heritage, it gave me the courage to believe that as long as we remained committed to family, we would find a way to endure every trial life might bring.

Convinced by our memories and experience that there is a richness and holiness in every household, my colleague, Father Jack Rathschmidt, and I offer this small book as a path to uncovering the wonder and wisdom of family and faith gatherings. Almost everyone we know, with a little prodding, can remember rituals from their childhood that not only gave them a deep sense of belonging to family, but also offered them a way of saying who they were.

People all over the world celebrate rituals to mark solstices and equinoxes, holidays and holy days, births, marriages, anniversaries and death and other life milestones. Rituals allow us to remember our past, hope for the future, live in the now and mark important events, no matter how painful, as celebrations of human becoming and faith.

Light is an especially important dimension of life and these celebrations. Who of us does not know the gratitude we feel as dawn comes after an especially difficult night or the joy of lighting birthday candles for children and adults alike? That is why we invite you to light two candles during each of the rituals found in this book. Honoring the past and hoping for a faith-filled future through the gesture of lighting candles offers us a way to live our faith fully in the present.

Using Prayer-Celebrations

We created the 58 prayer-celebrations in *The Blessing Candles* primarily for families, but the rituals also can be used effectively to begin meetings with larger groups and other faith gatherings. In our experience, these prayer-celebrations work best when they precede or follow a meal.

Each ritual takes ten minutes or less, depending upon how much time you allow for reflection on the questions provided. If you have a hot meal waiting or people on strict time schedules, you may want to keep discussion brief!

Each blessing ritual consists of seven elements: Symbol, Gathering Prayer, Two Candles, Reading, Questions for Reflection, Response and Sending Prayer.

> The **Symbol** is an item easily found in most homes and that fits on a table. The symbol, representing the past, is a visual connection to the theme of the ritual. Feel free to substitute your own symbols.

> The **Gathering Prayer** calls everyone together for a short prayer to set the tone and begin the ritual.

> Next comes the lighting of **Two Candles**—one to represent the past and one to represent the future.

> The **Reading** is a short citation from Scripture or an appropriate work of literature, a prayer or inspirational quote. Again, feel free to substitute a reading that speaks well to your family or group.

Following the Reading, if time permits, you will find several **Questions for Reflection** that provide opportunity for faith-sharing.

Each **Response** is a prayerful petition that invites those gathered to pray aloud together.

The rituals conclude with a **Sending Prayer** that sums up the ritual and sends forth those gathered.

Getting Started

We offer these guidelines to help you get started using *The Blessing Candles* and to feel comfortable with mealtime rituals.

1. **Prepare the space** where people will gather so that all can sit, preferably in a circle around a simply adorned table. Bring focus to the center of the table by placing on it a cloth, a place mat or a doily. When we pay attention to our prayer space, we are symbolically attending to the sacred within ourselves and our world. At times you might choose to play soft music to further enhance the environment.

2. **Place two candles,** symbolic of the past and future, on the table and have matches available.

    The selection of candle holders can enhance the celebration. Homemade holders, wedding gifts, gifts from deceased family members and holders from other cultures can help everyone focus on the prayer of the day without using too many words.

    Colored candles or colored ribbons tied around candles can help reflect the theme, the mood or the season.

    Encourage whoever lights the candles to take his or her time. Striking a match can remind all to be and bring light to everyone.

    Be watchful during the lighting, burning and extinguishing of the candles so that fire does not endanger anyone present.

3. **Place the symbol** between the two candles on the cloth. The symbol represents the present and is mentioned at the

beginning of each ritual. We recommend certain symbols for each prayer service, but you should feel free to choose your own or place greens to represent the present.

4. **Choose a leader** to call all to prayerful attention. When children are present, they can ring a gong or bell to get people's attention and signal the time to gather.

5. **Ask different people, even children, to read** each section to foster variety and participation. For each ritual you will find poems, stories, quotations, Scriptures and readings from other cultures. Again, you should feel free to substitute readings that fit better your particular circumstances.

6. **Use simple gestures**. We offer breathing prayers, silence and a number of closing gestures. Gestures help everyone become involved and often are the only way many people feel free to express themselves.

7. **Shorten the rituals when necessary but always light the two candles**—one candle to represent the past and a second candle, the future. Pause after lighting each candle. A few moments of silence invites people to enter the prayer personally.

8. **The questions after the readings** encourage further quiet reflection and, when time permits, foster the sharing of life and faith experiences, explaining awards and symbols, and give people a chance to express what this ritual really means to them. We offer these questions especially for prayer before meetings, for groups like the RCIA and for special occasions.

9. **Honor the gathering space** and the symbols and actions used there by first celebrating the ritual, "Blessing and Dedication of Two Candles," found on page 8.

10. **Improvise** to fit your situation as you become more comfortable with prayer and ritual and the people gathered.

11. **Remember that gentle prayer can transform** people, families and groups.

Becoming Lights of Faith, Beacons of Hope

Our prayer is simple: Do not be afraid of the past. Light a candle to it and let its pain drift away and its glory glow. And do not fear the future. The light of faith will always be a beacon of hope to all who follow it. Most of all, be alive to the present. That is where God lives and moves. May *The Blessing Candles* enrich your prayer life and your family life, and bring you closer to the Light of the world, Jesus Christ!

Gaynell Bordes Cronin
Jack Rathschmidt, O.F.M. Cap.

The Blessing Candles

Blessing and Dedication of Two Candles

Symbol

Bowl of water with green sprig from tree or bush

Gathering Prayer

God of All Time and Place, we gather to recognize and acknowledge your presence living within and among us in the sacredness of the ordinary: moment by moment, day by day, month by month, year by year. You call us from our busy lives to spend time with you and with one another. May this be our gathering and blessing place. Welcome!

Two Candles

In dedication, we bless our candle to the past. In this lighting may we remember we are never alone. We have a history, a heritage, a connection to people who have walked before us in faith.

Light one candle. Be silent.

In dedication, we bless our candle to the future. In this lighting may we be challenged with the dream and hope of who we can become as one people of God, brothers and sisters to one another.

Light second candle. Be silent.

And in this sacred time of the now, the present, we pray to be honest about who we are in our strengths and weaknesses, our joys and sadness, with gratitude and thanksgivings.

Pause.

Reading

Listen to the wisdom of Psalms:

> Your word is a lamp to my feet and a light to my path. *(119:105)*

Response

Our response is "Blessed be God forever."

Blessed are you, Lord our God, for giving us candles to burn. *Response*

Blessed are you, Lord our God, for giving us matches that kindle flame. *Response*

Blessed are you, Lord our God, for giving us this gathering table. *Response*

Blessed are you, Lord our God, for giving us people to celebrate your love. *Response*

Blessed are you, Lord our God, for giving us stories to hear and tell. *Response*

Sending Prayer

Make us light to one another. In your light, may we be light and know your presence in all the actions of our daily living.

Dip green sprig into water and bless each object and each person with the sprig.

Blessings for Everyday

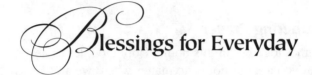

ℬlessing for Home

Symbol

Empty chair at tableside

Gathering Prayer

As we gather together in this home, Holy God, let us never forget that you are our home no matter where we are. Bless all those who are homeless.

Two Candles

For all those who taught us that our homes are sacred places.

Light one candle. Be silent.

For all those who will work to build holy homes in the future.

Light second candle. Be silent.

For all who are gathered here. May we be a welcoming home for one another.

Pause.

Reading

Saint Teresa of Avila reminds us:

> In this house, all must be friends,
> all must be loved, all must be held dear,
> all must be helped.[1]

Questions for Reflection

How can we make our home a place where people feel welcome?

When have you felt especially welcomed at home?

Response

Our response is "Be our home, O God."

Whenever we are lost. *Response*

Whenever we welcome others. *Response*

Wherever we are. *Response*

When we feel separated from family and friends. *Response*

For what else shall we pray? *Pause, then response*

Sending Prayer

God of Homes and the Homeless, be our home. Bless our home. May your peace and joy abide here.

All say: Amen.

May your goodness and mercy live here.

All say: Amen.

May your calm light of patience and courage shine here.

All say: Amen.

And may we always welcome you and all people into our homes, Holy One, in a spirit of love and hospitality. We ask this in your name, God, the Light of our home life.

All say: Amen.

As we stand by this empty chair, let us name someone we would like to welcome: _____.

*B*lessing for Vehicles

Symbol

Vehicle key

Gathering Prayer

The freedom to travel is a great gift, God of Roads and Byways. As we gather, we thank you especially for this vehicle, *(name it)* _____. May we be safe in our travel. Help us not only to get from place to place, but to enjoy your creation along the way.

Two Candles

For all who taught us to delight in travel and recreation.

Light one candle. Be silent.

May the people of tomorrow always honor the roads and resources of the earth.

Light second candle. Be silent.

May the use of _____ be a source of great pleasure and enjoyment.

Pause.

Reading

Author Kent Nerburn writes:

> ...We need to travel. If we don't offer ourselves to the unknown, our senses dull. Our world becomes small and we lose our sense of wonder. Our eyes don't lift to the horizon; our ears don't hear the sounds around us. The

edge is off our experience... We wake up one day and find that we have lost our dreams in order to protect our days. Don't let yourself become one of these people.[2]

Questions for Reflection

How would you like to use this vehicle to help others?

Where do you dream of traveling? What would you like to see or do?

Response

Our response is "Keep us safe, Protector God."

In all our travels. *Response*

When we are alone. *Response*

In this vehicle _____. *Response*

With our family and friends. *Response*

For what else shall we pray? *Pause, then response*

Sending Prayer

The joy of having this vehicle _____ is great, O God. Travel with us, keep us safe and help us to remember to sing and shout your name wherever we go. Amen.

Turn and bless the four directions of travel—east, west, north, south.

*B*lessing for Work

Symbol

Bricks

Gathering Prayer

Honest work offers us simple dignity, God of Work and Workers. We are immensely grateful for it. Help us consider our attitude in accepting and doing simple tasks around our homes. Never let us forget how privileged we are to help and serve others in the works we do.

Two Candles

For all those whose work-filled lives helped us value having a job that provided us with food, solace and freedom.

Light one candle. Be silent.

For all those whose labor will offer life and growth for the people of tomorrow.

Light second candle. Be silent.

Encouraged by those who worked hard and hopeful about those who will follow us, we pray in gratitude for the work we will do today.

Pause.

Reading

Poet T. S. Eliot wrote:

> In the vacant places
> We will build with new bricks

There are hands and machines
And clay for new brick
And lime for new mortar
Where the bricks are fallen
We will build with new stone.
Where the beams are rotten
We will build with new timbers
Where the word is unspoken
We will build with new speech
There is work together
A church for all
And a job for each
Every man to his work. [3]

Questions for Reflection

Do you think most people like and enjoy their work?

What can we do to help others enjoy work?

Response

How wonderful, O God, to have and to enjoy our work. With our hands, hearts and minds, we strive as family to help bring order to our world and home. Be present with us in the works we do today.

Invite all to mention a work for which they would like to pray.

Sending Prayer

God of Work and Occupations, bless us with strength and faithfulness in the work we do. We promise to help create a new world and to thank people for all they do. We ask this in your name, God, Maker of all Creation. Amen.

Ask all to bow their heads in gratitude for the work they do.

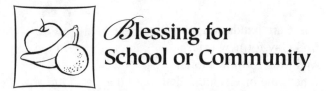

Blessing for School or Community

Symbol

Fruits

Gathering Prayer

How fortunate we are, God of Wisdom, for a place and a community in which to learn. Empower us to bless our school and community with a commitment to honest and free inquiry. Be our guardian and protector as we learn, live and search for the truth.

Two Candles

For all those who have pursued education and reminded us of the privilege of learning together.

Light one candle. Be silent.

For the children of tomorrow, challenged by the enormous explosion of information available to them.

Light second candle. Be silent.

May all gathered here rejoice in the wonder and awe of learning.

Pause.

Reading

Author Megan McKenna recounts this story:

> There was once an old Jewish man. All he ever did in his spare time was go to the edge of the village and plant fig trees. "You are going to die before you can eat any of the

fruit that they produce," [the people said]. But he said, "I have spent so many happy hours sitting under fig trees and eating their fruit. Those trees were planted by others. Why shouldn't I make sure that others will know the enjoyment that I have had?"[4]

Questions for Reflection

What makes a school a good learning place?

How can you make this school a better community?

Response

Our response is "Amen."

May we eat the fruit of trees planted by our teachers, mentors, parents and grandparents. *Response*

May we plant fig trees for others. *Response*

May we go to the edge of the village, school and community of _____ searching for truth and wisdom. *Response*

Sending Prayer

God of Knowledge and Learning, let us leave this place and people determined to enrich the world with what we learn and with whom we become. We stretch our hands toward this school and community, palms up, in a silent blessing. Amen.

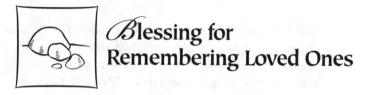

Blessing for Remembering Loved Ones

Symbol

A stone

Gathering Prayer

Never let us forget, God of Memory, how much you and all those who have walked with us in life love us. Stop us when we forget and challenge us to remember your care.

Two Candles

May the goodness of those who walked ahead of us never be forgotten.

Light one candle. Be silent.

May we be held in the memory of those who will walk after us.

Light second candle. Be silent.

May those with us be blessed as we remember and welcome the spirits of the people who have gone before us: relatives, friends and guests.

Pause.

Reading

Listen to the wisdom from the Book of Genesis:

> [God said:] "Know that I am with you; I will protect you wherever you go, and bring you back to this land. I will never leave you until I have done what I promised you."

> When Jacob awoke from his sleep, he exclaimed, "Truly, the Lord is in this spot, although I did not know it!"...

Jacob then made this vow: "If God remains with me, to protect me on this journey I am making…, the Lord shall be my God. This stone that I have set up as a memorial stone shall be God's abode."[5] *(28:15, 16, 20-22)*

Questions for Reflection

How do you stay aware of God's presence wherever you go?

What is your most special memory of a friend or family member?

Response

Our response is "Pray for us."

We pray as your family, Loving God.
As the communion of saints,
we join with all who have gone before us,
those now living and those yet to live.
Holy Mary, Mother of God. *Response*

All grandparents and great-grandparents. *Response*

All relatives and friends. *Response*

All holy men and women. *Response*

All the saints and holy people whose names we bear. *Response*

All who worked for truth, justice and freedom. *Response*

For whom else shall we pray? *Pause, then response*

Sending Prayer

Free us to be a blessing for all your people, O God. Let those who have forgotten your promise to be present among us always, find you in us. As we pass the memorial stone to one another, we say: Remember and be holy, _____ *(name)*. Amen.

Pass the stone from person to person and repeat last phrase of Sending Prayer.

ℬlessing for Creation

Symbol

Nuts

Gathering Prayer

Loving God, your presence and care gently permeate all creation. Like a star burst, a sunrise, a stone or the ocean, you fill us with hope and awe. Gather us now as we attend to the wonder of all your gifts.

Two Candles

In gratitude for all that is and all who formed us in awe and wonder.

Light one candle. Be silent.

In hope that all our tomorrows will be filled with gratitude for creation.

Light second candle. Be silent.

And for all here gathered, may we see, hear, smell, touch and rejoice again in all God's gifts of wind, water, fire and earth.

Pause.

Reading

The mystic Julian of Norwich wrote:

> And in this he showed me something small, no bigger than a hazelnut, lying in the palm of my hand, as it seemed to me, and it was as round as a ball. I looked at it with the eye of my understanding and thought: What can

this be? I was amazed that it could last, for I thought that because of its littleness it would suddenly have fallen into nothing. And I was answered in my understanding: It lasts and always will, because God loves it; and thus everything has being through the love of God.[6]

Questions for Reflection

What is your favorite example of the beauty of creation (a sunset, ocean, mountains, flower garden, bird)?

How can we show our respect and reverence for God's creation?

Response

Our response is "We give you thanks, Creator God."

For stars, sky, moon and sun. *Response*

For water, earth, fire and wind. *Response*

For friends and family. *Response*

For all who challenge us to grow in love of creation. *Response*

For what else shall we be grateful? *Pause, then response*

Sending Prayer

You are at the center of all that is, O God. You are our breath and our life. You are our hope and love. Send us as servants of all that is and teach us to honor all you have given us. Amen.

Please take and carry a nut today as a reminder to ask God for a deeper appreciation of creation.

ℬlessing for Care of the Earth

Symbol

Small trowel

Gathering Prayer

How beautiful and wondrous is your creation, Creator God. How marvelous are your works! Pour the fullness of your creative energy into us as we gather to reflect and pray about the grandeur of your work.

Two Candles

For farmers, farm workers and gardeners. For all who love, cultivate and care for the earth.

Light one candle. Be silent.

For tomorrow's children who will continue the work of creation.

Light second candle. Be silent.

May we here gathered recommit ourselves to preserve, guard, protect and care for our earth.

Pause.

Reading

From the United Nations, we read:

> "Great Spirit, give us hearts to understand; never to take from creation's beauty more than we give, never to destroy wantonly for the furtherance of greed; never to deny to give our hands for the building of earth's beauty. Never

to take from her what we cannot use... that as we care for her she will care for us."[7] Amen.

Questions for Reflection

What does creation mean to you?

How can we care for creation more completely?

Response

You call us, Gift-Giving God, to have a marvelous relationship with the earth.

Our response is "Your gift of earth belongs to everyone, Creator God."

May we care for rivers, seas, oceans, ponds, brooks, streams and lakes, remembering. *Response*

May we plant fruit-bearing trees, vegetables, vineyards, orchards, flowers, fields of grain, remembering. *Response*

May we preserve the freshness of clean air, the smells of early morning dew, the scents of changing seasons, remembering. *Response*

Sending Prayer

Help us care for the earth, Creator God, like you nourish us: gently, strongly, faithfully. As you awaken us to the grandeur of all creation, give us feet to walk humbly and hands to touch tenderly the gifts of this garden earth. Amen.

Exchange a sign of peace saying, "May you reawaken a spirit of thoughtfulness for the earth."

Blessing for Friendship

Symbol

Telephone

Gathering Prayer

You, O God, are our gentle friend. Gift us with friendship.
Open our thirsting spirits to find you in all our friendships.

Two Candles

God of Friendship, we joyfully remember all those who have
walked with us as friends.

Light one candle. Be silent.

In the light of our second candle, may we recognize those called
to be friends in the future.

Light second candle. Be silent.

And in the present we rest, grateful for the friends we have
today. We mention them by name: _____.

Pause

Reading

Listen to the wisdom of our Hindu friends:

> Strong One, make me strong. May all beings look on me
> with the eye of a friend! May I look on all beings with the
> eye of a friend! May we look on one another with the eye
> of a friend.[8]

Questions for Reflection

What is your best experience of friendship?

What are the most important aspects of being a friend to others?

Response

Imagine placing your friends in your open hands as we sit in silence honoring them.

We pray, Holy Friend, for the gift of enduring friendship. Preserve our present friendships. Fill us, challenge us to open the doors of our hearts to new ones. Let us not be afraid to share our hearts and lives in friendship. May the friends you send help us to become who you would have us be.

Sending Prayer

Bless, O God, with the fruits of love, all your people, especially those most in need of a simple friendship. Bless our friends with lasting hope, deep honesty and new life. Bless them also with our love. May we be good friends to all. Amen.

Ask all to raise and extend open hands in blessing of friends.

𝒷lessing for Peace

Symbol

Potted plant

Gathering Prayer

Challenge us again, O God, to be peacemakers at home, in our neighborhoods, our parishes and our world. Help us to think first of reconciliation, not anger and division. With you, Peacemaking God, we can create a new world where lasting peace rooted in justice reigns.

Two Candles

In gratitude to all peacemakers who have gone before us: relatives and friends, teachers and mentors, Saints Francis and Clare of Assisi, Mahatma Gandhi, Martin Luther King, Jr., and Dorothy Day, and all who lived peaceful lives. We name the peacemakers in our lives: _____ *(names).*

Light one candle. Be silent.

For all those who will be challenged to make peace in the twenty-first century. May they be strengthened by our faith to walk gently on the earth and make it a place where all share earth's abundant blessings.

Light second candle. Be silent.

And between the past and future we rest, committed to be peaceful with one another today.

Pause.

Reading

A video called *Peace* tells us:

> Be a maker of peace and make gentle the ways of this
> world. Walk in peace. Work in peace. Live in peace.
> Be with another in peace. Be with yourself in peace.
> Be active as peace is active, in doing something, making
> something, in becoming one with God and one with all
> the people God has made.[9]

Questions for Reflection

Who is the most peaceful person you know? What qualities did
the person have?

When do you feel peaceful?

Response

Fill us, O God, with peace and teach us to be peacemakers in the
world. May we plant the seeds of peace and nourish their growth
by the way we live with others. We trust that your peace will fill
us to overflowing and will allow us to create a new world.

Sending Prayer

Please stand.

Leader: Peace be with you.

All: And also with you.

Leader: May the peace of Christ reign in your hearts.

All: And also in your heart.

Leader: Send us now, Gracious God, into the world as agents of
peace and let each word we speak *(touch mouth)* and step we
take *(take step)* bring your peace to all we meet. Amen.

Ask all to offer a sign of peace.

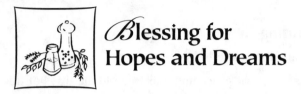

*B*lessing for Hopes and Dreams

Symbol

Spices

Gathering Prayer

Bring us together again, Gatherer God, so that we might reflect on all our hopes and dreams. You have assured us that we could pray for anything in your name. Listen to us now.

Two Candles

For all who have lived their dreams and encouraged us to have ours.

Light one candle. Be silent.

For all children, may they never be afraid to hope and dream.

Light second candle. Be silent.

For all here gathered, may we listen to our dreams again today as we share them with one another: _____.

Pause.

Reading

Rabbi Susya used to say:

> If they ask me in the next world, "Why were you not Moses?" I will know the answer. But if they ask me, "Why were you not Susya?" I will have nothing to say.[10]

Questions for Reflection

What is your most important dream?

What help do you need to move toward making it come true?

Response

You ask us, O God, only to be ourselves. But how hard that is when we live with broken and bruised dreams. Kindle and warm our hope to live each day fully. There is, we know, no other way to realize and accept your dreams for us.

Sending Prayer

We are ready to move again, Challenging God. Help us not to be afraid of our dreams. Let us gently prod all those who have abandoned themselves, their hopes and their faith. Through the aroma of these spices, awaken our courage to speak of who we are through the works we do and the dreams we share.

Pass and smell spices.

*B*lessing for Kindness

Symbol
Jar of honey

Gathering Prayer
How kind, how gentle, you are to us, God of Loving Kindness. Even when we turn our hearts from you, you continue to wait for our glance to rest on you again. Strengthen us with the courage to be kind even when it hurts.

Two Candles
For all those who have shown us kindness.

Light one candle. Be silent.

For all those who will be challenged to be kind in the future.

Light second candle. Be silent.

And in the present, we speak of ways to offer kindness to one another.

Share ways: _____.

Pause.

Reading
The prophet Muhammad wrote:

> What actions are excellent? To gladden the heart of a human being. To feed the hungry. To help the afflicted. To lighten the sorrow of the sorrowful. To remove the wrongs of the injured. That person is the most beloved of God who does most good to God's creatures.[11]

Questions for Reflection

When has someone been kind to you?

Do we have a duty to show others kindness, even those we dislike?

Response

To be kind is a simple command but often a difficult challenge. Help us, God of All Kindness, not to be afraid of your command to love, not just our neighbors, but even our enemies. Give us courage to do random acts of kindness and senseless acts of beauty. And let us never forget your bottomless goodness to us.

Sending Prayer

With the breath of your spirit emboldening us, O God, we believe that we can learn to show kindness for your people even when we do not feel kind. Send us with strength, free us from fear of hurt and let the spirit's breath touch all with hope. Nourish us with foods to walk the path of kindness. Amen.

Give each person a spoon. Ask each person to dip spoon into honey jar and eat.

Blessing for Patience

Symbol

Blades of grass

Gathering Prayer

Anger, worry and anxiety often get in the way of our authentic selves. As we come together to pray today, Patient God, calm our restless need for quick answers and easy solutions. Free us of all that interferes with our desire to care for your creatures and open our hearts to patient waiting for growth and the fullness of life.

Two Candles

In gratitude for all people who tolerated us when we were intolerable.

Light one candle. Be silent.

For the children of tomorrow, may they never lose patience with themselves or others.

Light second candle. Be silent.

For all here gathered, may we learn to take life one step at a time.

Pause.

Reading

Henry Miller wrote:

> The moment one gives close attention to anything, even a blade of grass, it becomes a mysterious, awesome, indescribably magnificent world in itself.[12]

Questions for Reflection

Who is the most patient person you know?

What do you do to remain patient at difficult times?

Response

When we feel great stress, patience can seem impossible. We want to do something, not because it is right, but to escape our anxiety. Patient God, let us look at a blade of grass today so that its mystery and awesome wonder might help us not to run so fast that even you can't find us.

Sending Prayer

Be persistent with us, O God. Do not turn your back when we rush ahead to act as if we were you. Fill us with patience and endurance as we try to bring good news to others. Amen.

Offer a sign of encouragement to others by saying:

_____ *(Name)*, be patient with all that is unresolved in your heart.

ℬlessing
for Gratitude

Symbol

T-shirt

Gathering Prayer

We are so grateful, O Good and Generous God, for all you are and all you give us. As we gather to thank you, make us even more aware of the wonder of your care. Enfold us in the garment of your love.

Two Candles

In gratitude for all those who have walked in faith before us.

Light one candle. Be silent.

For all who will seek to live grateful lives after us.

Light second candle. Be silent.

And may we express each day our gratitude to God and one another.

Pause.

Reading

In the Book of Colossians, we read:

> As God's chosen ones, holy and beloved, clothe yourselves with compassion, kindness, humility, meekness, and patience. Bear with one another and, if anyone has a complaint against another, forgive each other; just as the Lord has forgiven you...Above all, clothe yourselves with

love, which binds everything together in perfect harmony. *(3:12-14)*

Questions for Reflection

For which person are you most grateful in your life today?

How do you feel when someone thanks you?

Response

Good and Generous God, we clothe ourselves in gratitude as your people.

Mention all present as you move through the following prayer.

You are kind and compassionate, _____.

You are humble and gentle, _____.

_____, you get along easily with others.

_____, you are peaceful.

_____, you help others.

And _____, you sing with a glad heart.

Sending Prayer

Shake us gently out of our complacency, God, and remind us that we are to be your body on earth. Let all who come to us hungry, leave grateful for having met you through us. Amen.

Ask all to join hands in a circle of gratitude.

ℬlessing for Acceptance

Symbol

A calendar

Gathering Prayer

Sometimes, God of All Days and Years, we struggle with accepting and walking the path you set before us. As we gather in faith, give us the courage to hand ourselves over to you again with complete trust.

Two Candles

For all those whose accepting natures taught us trust.

Light one candle. Be silent.

For all those who will need to accept difficult days in the future.

Light second candle. Be silent.

For all gathered here today, may we trust and accept God's will for us as we acknowledge our own imperfections.

Pause.

Reading

Saint Thérèse of Lisieux, the Little Flower of Jesus, wrote:

> Ordinary Folk, like you and me, must be greatly loved by God since there are so many of us, always have been, most likely always will be...Our faults cannot hurt God. Nor will our failures interfere with our own holiness... (for) genuine holiness is precisely a matter of enduring our own imperfections patiently.[13]

Questions for Reflection

What do you think is the key to self-acceptance, to liking the person you are?

How can we help other people accept themselves as they are before God?

Response

Our response is "Help us let go, God of Life."

Keep your hands open on your lap.

When we cling to our own fears. *Response*

When we cling to our own ways. *Response*

When we fail to listen to others. *Response*

When we fail to listen to you. *Response*

For what else shall we pray? *Pause, then response*

Sending Prayer

Sometimes, Trusting God, we let go only for a moment. Today, help us let go completely and like Saint Thérèse, the Little Flower of Jesus, trust your great and unconditional love for us. In all calendar days and years, may our desire to live in you be a blessing to others.

Let us breathe in and say: Trust.

Pause.

Let us breathe out and say: Let go.

Pause.

Amen.

Blessing for Solidarity

Symbol

World map

Gathering Prayer

Too often, God of Oneness, we are separated from one another and you unnecessarily. Unite us today and, as we gather, let us experience your deep yearning that we might welcome all people as friends.

Two Candles

For all who have worked for unity in the world.

Light one candle. Be silent.

For all who will work for world peace and solidarity tomorrow.

Light second candle. Be silent.

For all gathered here. May we be at one with all creation.

Pause.

Reading

Listen to the wisdom of Nelson Mandela:

> The time for healing of the wounds has come...
> There is no easy road to freedom...
> None of us acting alone can achieve success.
> We must therefore act together as a unified people,
> for reconciliation, for nation building, for the birth of
> a new world.[14]

Questions for Reflection

When have you met someone from another culture, someone whose daily life is very different from yours? What was this person like?

Who do you admire in the world who works for world peace?

Response

Our response is "Make us one, God of Unity."

When we are at odds with one another. *Response*

When we threaten others with harm. *Response*

When we are afraid to defend the weak because of the anger of the strong. *Response*

When we support governments that unjustly use violence. *Response*

For what else shall we pray? *Pause, then response*

Sending Prayer

Help us to see good in others, God of Solidarity, as we work to create a world where all people respect one another. Let us dream, work and pray together. Amen.

Hold hands with those beside you to form a circle. Imagine giving and receiving strength to one another. Open hands and turn to four directions sending everyone a blessing of strength and oneness.

𝒷lessing for Courage

Symbol

A sweater

Gathering Prayer

Give us your strength, Peaceful God, as we gather. Help us remember all you have done for us. With your help, all is possible. Let us breathe in and say: fear not.

Pause.

Let us breathe out and say: I am here.

Pause.

Two Candles

For all those who have strengthened us with courage.

Light one candle. Be silent.

For all those who will need courage in the future.

Light second candle. Be silent.

For all of us here, may we be a source of courage for one another.

Pause.

Reading

Saint Catherine of Siena wrote powerfully:

> I, the sea of peace...
> Share with you, with each of you
> according to your own capacity.

I fill you
and do not leave you empty.[15]

Questions for Reflection

Who do you think has lots of courage?

What stops us from being courageous?

Response

Our response is "Wrap us with courage, God."

When we are troubled and lost. *Response*

When we walk into the unfamiliar. *Response*

When we are afraid of what tomorrow may bring. *Response*

When the dark seems overwhelming. *Response*

For what else shall we pray? *Pause, then response*

Sending Prayer

Wherever we go, O God, we trust you are with us. Wrap a sweater of courage around us. Send us with the strength to overcome all our fears and worries and fill us with a deep sense of Jesus' courage in facing life and death. Amen.

Ask each person to accept this sweater of courage. Place it around one person's shoulders and then ask that person to pass it to the next person until all have worn the sweater of courage.

Blessing for Good Health

Symbol

Apple and small bowl of water

Gathering Prayer

What a great gift health is, God of Life. How we struggle when we are sick. As we gather today, make us aware of the unity of our body and spirit. Remind us again of your healing touch and teach us to care for ourselves and one another.

Two Candles

For all those people who taught us that good health is one of God's great gifts: _____ *(Name people)*.

Light one candle. Be silent.

For all who may struggle with poor health.

Light second candle. Be silent.

For all gathered here. May we recommit ourselves to care gently for our health.

Pause.

Reading

Listen to the wisdom and wit of Martin Buber:

> A story must be told in such a way that it constitutes help in itself. My grandfather was lame. Once they asked him to tell a story about his teacher and he related how his teacher used to hop and dance while he prayed. My grandfather rose as he spoke, and he was so swept away

by his story that he began to hop and dance and show how the master had done. From that hour he was cured of his lameness. That's how to tell a story.[16]

Questions for Reflection

What makes a person healthy?

How can we support good health in one another?

Response

Our response is "So be it."

May laughter and affection lighten our moods. *Response*

May music and silence lift our spirits. *Response*

May hopping and dancing soothe our broken dreams. *Response*

May hearing and telling stories awaken our zest for life. *Response*

May health, food, water and exercise nourish our bodies. *Response*

Sending Prayer

God, Source of Life and Sustenance, may we never take for granted your daily care for us. Make us grateful for the wholeness of life and the gift of good health. Let us be a healing presence to all we meet. To promote our good health this week, we will _____.

Cut apple horizontally to reveal the seeds in a five-sided star shape, a sign of timelessness. Dip apple slice in water and eat for health all our days.

*B*lessing for Managing Finances

Symbol

Money

Gathering Prayer

The call to good stewardship of our finances and property, Generous God, is a challenging one. Help us as we gather to reflect on our faithfulness and caring in the wise management of our finances.

Two Candles

In gratitude for all those who have cared for us financially.

Light one candle. Be silent.

May our children have the resources to care for one another.

Light second candle. Be silent.

May all of us be grateful for the goods and money we have.

Pause.

Reading

Jacob Needleman writes:

> If I had to say what I think the role of money is in human life, I would say that one needs money to live and survive in the outer world, to fulfill one's obligations to the community and to nature, but that above and beyond this, the role of money is to serve as the instrument for getting understanding.[17]

Questions for Reflection

Have you ever felt poor? How did you react?

How can we help one another live simply and justly?

Response

Our response is "Guiding Spirit, give us wisdom."

Disputes about money and unpaid bills can weaken families. *Response*

Arguments over when, what and how much to buy can divide people. *Response*

Overspending, preoccupation with possessions and owning at the expense of others can foster greed. *Response*

For what else shall we pray? *Pause, then response*

Sending Prayer

Help and guide us in your Spirit, God, never to take for granted the things we have. Teach us also to be generous servants of those most in need. Amen.

Invite all to ask forgiveness for the times we have not been good stewards of our finances.

$\mathcal{B}$lessings for Special Needs

𝒷lessing for Career Decisions

Symbol

A flower

Gathering Prayer

Guiding God, all of us must make difficult decisions in our life. Sometimes these moments can fill us with a kind of dread that keeps us from paying attention to you and one another. As we gather today, help us listen well to your voice of wisdom and direction.

Two Candles

We light a candle to all those whose gentle counsel helped us in the past.

Light one candle. Be silent.

We light a candle to all those who will need wise guidance in the future.

Light a second candle. Be silent.

Between these candles we rest, secure in the conviction that you will always guide our lives and be our strength in making every career decision.

Reading

Wu-Men, a Chinese poet, writes:

> Ten thousand flowers in spring,
> the moon in autumn,
> a cool breeze in summer,

snow in winter.
If your mind isn't clouded by
unnecessary things,
this is the best season of your life.[18]

Questions for Reflection

How do you make decisions in your life?

What is the best thing others can do to help you make decisions?

Response

Our response is "Guide us, Gentle God."

Through all our decisions. *Response*

As we uncloud our mind from unnecessary worry. *Response*

As we decide how best to serve you. *Response*

For all those who resist your help. *Response*

For what else shall we pray? *Pause, then response*

Sending Prayer

We trust in your providence, God of All Directions. Let us never forget that even as we seek new paths in life, you are with us. Help us speak of your love with every step we take. Amen.

Ask someone to sing or read this American Shaker song as you all move in a circle clockwise.

'Tis the gift to be simple, 'tis the gift to be free, 'tis the gift to come down where you ought to be, And when we find ourselves in the place just right, It will be in the valley of love and delight. *Repeat*

*B*lessing When Leaving or Losing a Job

Symbol

Wind chimes

Gathering Prayer

Sometimes, God of Life and Hope, fear fills us. We lose or leave a job, and the anxiety of not knowing what we will do or where we will go overwhelms us. Help us as we gather to support one another at this difficult time. We trust that you will always sustain us.

Two Candles

For all those who encouraged us to work, to pursue our goals, to strive to live well without undue competition.

Light one candle. Be silent.

For all those who will seek work, may they find it and you.

Light second candle. Be silent.

May all who are gathered here, especially _____ *(name),* who has left a job, know your strength and support.

Pause.

Reading

Listen to the wisdom of our Native American sisters and brothers:

> O Great Spirit, whose voice I hear in the winds and whose breath gives life to all the world, hear me. I am small and weak. I need your strength and wisdom.[19]

Questions for Reflection

How can we support someone we know who loses a job?

If you lost a job, what would you want others to do for you?

Response

Our response is "Help us, God of Our Life."

For all without work. *Response*

For all seeking work. *Response*

For all who doubt their abilities. *Response*

For all who support us in need. *Response*

For what else shall we pray? *Pause, then response*

Sending Prayer

Help us today, O God, to trust you with our lives. Continue to breathe your life in us. Though we are afraid and often worried about what tomorrow will bring, we know that you are with us. Show us the path to life and hope and be our God of New Beginnings.

Ask everyone to sit quietly for a moment with hands open in their laps.

Let us breathe in and say: I am.

Let us breathe out and say: your life. Amen.

*B*lessing When Choosing a New School or College

Symbol

Book

Gathering Prayer

Teacher God, we know that education is such an essential and integral dimension of life. Learning allows us not only to pursue work, it enhances our sense of ourselves. Guide us as we gather to know which school is best for _____ *(name)*.

Two Candles

For all who taught us the value of learning.

Light one candle. Be silent.

For all who will pursue education in the future.

Light second candle. Be silent.

In the present, we remember and share how education helped us.

Pause.

Reading

Listen to the wisdom of the Hindu tradition:

> Knowledge makes a person honest, virtuous, and endearing to society. It is learning alone that enables a person to better the condition of friends and relations. Knowledge is the holiest of holies, the god of the gods, and commands respect of crowned heads...The fixtures and furniture of one's house may be stolen by thieves, but knowledge, the highest treasure, is above all stealing.[20]

Questions for Reflection

What is most difficult about entering a new school?

What excites you about starting in a new school?

Response

Our response is "Help us, Teacher God."

So that all will appreciate learning and changing. *Response*

So that we might create a world where all can learn. *Response*

So that those who sacrifice so others can go to school will be rewarded. *Response*

So teachers everywhere will know how much we value them. *Response*

Sending Prayer

As we prepare to help _____ *(name)* leave one school, family and neighborhood to seek new horizons and pursue new dreams, let us together pray that each of us will learn something new each day simply by living well. Amen.

Ask all to open hands and welcome the newness of each day.

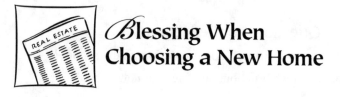

*B*lessing When Choosing a New Home

Symbol

Newspaper real estate ads

Gathering Prayer

Our homes say so much about us, Gracious God. They help us welcome friends, offer security to one another and provide a place to share our sacred stories. Help us as we gather to discern well how best we can live together.

Two Candles

For all those who provided shelter for us in the past.

Light one candle. Be silent.

For all who will seek homes in the future.

Light second candle. Be silent.

Seeking God's guidance about where to live, we speak of our dreams: _____.

Pause.

Reading

Noela Evans writes:

> The stage of my life has changed; old doors are closed and new ones now stand open. Though I may have seen this space before, I now come to make it mine, to call it home... I honor this place that will shelter me, and I embrace the changes and opportunities that this move invites into my life.[21]

Questions for Reflection

What excites you about living in a new home?

What frightens you?

Response

Our response is "Help us, Homemaking God."

For all who seek new homes, new apartments, new dreams. *Response*

For the homeless who need shelter and hope. *Response*

For all those who bring warmth into our lives. *Response*

For our own inner peace during anxious times. *Response*

For what else shall we pray? *Pause, then response*

Sending Prayer

Watch over us, Loving God, as we seek a secure place, a welcoming neighborhood and a warm community to call our own. Walk with us everywhere as we search. Help us to listen to your prompting and give us peace in all our wanderings. Amen.

Offer one another a sign of peace for the search.

*B*lessing When Disappointed

Symbol

Empty cup

Gathering Prayer

Loving God, we all experience loss in our life. We fail to live up to our own standards, we get sick, family and friends die. At times like this, we wonder where you are and why you do not help us. Let us enter into these disappointments today so that we might find your light again.

Let us breathe in and say: Love me.

Let us breathe out and say: Hold me.

Two Candles

In gratitude for all who taught us not to despair despite life's hurts.

Light one candle. Be silent.

In compassion for all who will struggle with disappointments in the future.

Light second candle. Be silent.

For all today trying to face their losses and grow in faith.

Pause.

Reading

Listen to the wisdom of Sidney Lovett:

> Every now and again take a good look at something not made with hands—a mountain, a star, the turn of a

stream. There will come to you wisdom and patience and solace and, above all, the assurance that you are not alone in the world.[22]

Questions for Reflection

How do you react to disappointments in your life?

How would you like to respond?

Response

Sometimes it is shame, O God, other times it is pride and anger that get in the way of our seeing you in every aspect of our lives. Help us not run from disappointments and loss. Strengthen us with faith. Let us never lose the hope that in you everything is possible.

Sending Prayer

Our shoulders are a bit rounded, Compassionate God, and though our faces are sad, we trust that you will lift our heavy burdens. Give us companions as we walk in darkness and fill our empty cup with the empathy that reminds us never to judge others. We trust that your light will come and find even the darkest places in our hearts. Amen.

Bow heads as empty cup is passed and held.

ℬlessing When Feelings Are Hurt

Symbol

Hand lotion

Gathering Prayer

We are feeling fragile and very vulnerable, O God, as we gather in faith. At a loss to know what to do with our hurt, help us to find your path for us.

Two Candles

For all who have known hurt and taught us not to despair.

Light one candle. Be silent.

For all who may know hurt tomorrow and not know what to do.

Light second candle. Be silent.

For all gathered here that we might support one another in our hurt: _____ *(Invite all to name hurt).*

Pause.

Reading

Listen to the wisdom of the Gospel of Saint Matthew:

> Blessed are the poor in spirit, for theirs is the kingdom of heaven.
>
> Blessed are those who mourn, for they will be comforted...
>
> Blessed are the peacemakers, for they will be called children of God...

Blessed are you when people revile you and persecute you and utter all kinds of evil against you falsely on my account. Rejoice and be glad, for your reward is great in heaven.... *(5:3-12)*

Questions for Reflection

How can we help others who are hurt?

How can we let others help us when we are hurt?

Response

Shout to us even more loudly, God of All Blessedness, about those you call blessed. Let us not forget your love for the poor, the mourning, the hungry, the peacemakers. As we acknowledge and speak honestly of our hurt feelings, heal us.

Ask people present to imagine placing their hurt feelings in their hands, holding them gently like a fragile newborn child.

Sending Prayer

Though we have been hurt, Loving God, we trust that your gentle touch will empower us to help heal others of hurt feelings. Amen.

Pass lotion and ask each person to rub it in their hands.

*B*lessing After Making Mistakes

Symbol

Piece of wood

Gathering Prayer

All of us make mistakes, Forgiving God. But sometimes, in order not to admit or accept our own, we focus on the mistakes of others. Help us as we gather not to let the "speck" in someone else's eye get in the way of seeing the "log" in our own.

Two Candles

In gratitude for all those who have admitted their mistakes and challenged us to accept our own.

Light one candle. Be silent.

For all those, especially our children, who will stumble in the future.

Light second candle. Be silent.

For all gathered here, may we face our mistakes today without fear.

Pause.

Reading

The Gospel of Saint Matthew asks us:

> Why do you see the speck in your neighbor's eye, but do not notice the log in your own eye? Or how can you say to your neighbor, "Let me take the speck out of your eye," while the log is in your own eye? You hypocrite, first take

the log out of your own eye, and then you will see clearly to take the speck out of your neighbor's eye. *(7:3-4)*

Questions for Reflection

Is it difficult to ask forgiveness when you make a mistake? What can we do for one another to make this task easier?

Response

Our response is "Help us, Forgiving God."

For all our mistakes. *Response*

For our smallness and blaming of others. *Response*

To be like those who forgive us. *Response*

For what else shall we pray? *Pause, then response*

Sending Prayer

Loving God, let us go peacefully into the world. Help us overcome our fear of admitting our mistakes. Let all those we meet feel the strength we have in accepting our weaknesses. Amen.

Place hands on shoulder of each person and say: Do not be afraid. Go in peace.

*B*lessing for Healing

Symbol

Olive oil

Gathering Prayer

You are our hope, Consoling God, in every trial. Gather us today and strengthen our faith as we come together to pray for healing in mind, body and spirit. We trust you will listen to our prayers.

Two Candles

For all in our past who accompanied us through illness and fear, who reminded us that darkness would pass and offered us a healing presence.

Light one candle. Be silent.

For our children and our children's children, may they never forget the healing power of God.

Light second candle. Be silent.

May God strengthen all here gathered against every physical, emotional and mental illness and fill us with

Breathe in and say: Strength.

Breathe out and say: Hope.

Reading

Listen to the Gospel of Saint Matthew:

> As Jesus went on from there, two blind men followed him, crying loudly, "Have mercy on us, Son of David!"

When he entered the house, the blind men came to him; and Jesus said to them, "Do you believe that I am able to do this?" They said to him, "Yes, Lord." Then he touched their eyes and said, "According to your faith let it be done to you." And their eyes were opened. *(9:27-30)*

Questions for Reflection

When have you felt healed?

How can you bring healing to others?

Response

Our response is "Free us, Healing Lord."

From all our fears. *Response*

From all our angers. *Response*

From all our lack of trust. *Response*

From all our sicknesses. *Response*

From what do you desire healing? *Pause, then response*

Sending Prayer

We are your children, O God, in need of your help. Touch us with compassion, fill us with hope and send us as healers to all those in need. Amen.

Ask all to imagine touching and smoothing their place of illness with the oil of healing.

*B*lessing for a Sick Person

Symbol

Bowl of water

Gathering Prayer

God of Compassion, you care for the sick and heal the brokenhearted. We open our hands to welcome your healing presence and ask your help especially for _____ *(name)*.

Two Candles

We light a candle to the past for all the people in our family and world who have cared for the sick and needy.

Light one candle. Be silent.

We light a candle to the future, that we might always walk with others in their need.

Light second candle. Be silent.

And in the present we name those people in our life who are sick: _____.

Pause.

Reading

Rabbi Rami Shapiro writes:

> There are moments when wellness escapes us. At such moments we must open ourselves to healing. May those whose lives are gripped in the palm of suffering open now to the Wonder of Life. May they discover through pain and torment the strength to live with humor. May they

discover through doubt and anguish the strength to live with dignity and holiness. May they discover through suffering and fear the strength to move toward healing.[23]

Questions for Reflection

When have you been asked to help someone who was sick?

What can you do when someone is sick?

Response

We pray for _____ *(name)* who is sick. Let your Spirit watch over _____ *(name)*. Give her/him strength to get well again. Help those who care for the sick everywhere: relatives, doctors, nurses, friends. Give them a healing touch. We dip our hands in water and make the Sign of the Cross on the hands of each family member.

Dip hands in water and make Sign of the Cross on each person present. If there is a large group, you may want to choose one or two people.

May your presence bring comfort to the sick. May your hands give loving care. Amen.

Sending Prayer

We extend our hands in blessing to _____ *(name)*.

May God the Father bless you. Amen.

May God the Son heal you. Amen.

May God the Holy Spirit strengthen you. Amen.

In the name of the Father, and of the Son, and of the Holy Spirit. Amen.

*B*lessing for Caregiving

Symbol

Stirring spoon

Gathering Prayer

Thank you, Tender and Loving God, for our family and loved ones, especially for those with special needs right now.
May they find strength and comfort in your love through us.
May we always be aware of the contributions they have made to our circle of family and loved ones.

Two Candles

For all in our family who cared for us when we were in need.

Light one candle. Be silent.

For all who will be challenged to offer a caring presence for family in the future.

Light second candle. Be silent.

May all of us gathered here be strong in our commitment to care for one another.

Pause.

Reading

Robert Johnson writes:

> Many years ago a wise friend gave me a name for human love. She called it "stirring the oatmeal" love...Stirring the oatmeal is a humble act...But it symbolizes a relatedness that brings love down to earth....Like the rice hulling of

the Zen monks, the spinning wheel of Gandhi, the tent making of St. Paul, it represents the discovery of the sacred in the midst of the humble and ordinary.[24]

Questions for Reflection

Has anyone in your family cared for you when you were sick or in need?

Have you been able to care for others? How did it feel?

Response

Our response is "Help us help one another."

With all our family cares. *Response*

With our service of those who are weak and most in need. *Response*

With our caring for all who are neglected. *Response*

For what else shall we pray? *Pause, then response*

Sending Prayer

We are your servants, Loving God. Give us "stirring the oatmeal love" for those needing special care and attention. May they know of your concern for them through us. Amen.

Pass the stirring spoon and invite all to name the care they will offer.

Blessing for a Pregnancy

Symbol

A wrapped gift

Gathering Prayer

Life is such a wonderful and precious gift, Loving God. As we gather to bless _____ *(name)*, let her know of your care deep in her heart. May we also grow in awe and wonder at your goodness in all of life.

Two Candles

For all who have given birth, may they always be our light.

Light one candle. Be silent.

For all who will give birth, may they be unafraid.

Light second candle. Be silent.

For all here gathered, may we never take life for granted.

Pause.

Reading

Author Eduardo Galeano writes:

> (When) Pilar and Daniel Weinberg's son was baptized... they gave him a sea shell. "So you'll learn to love the water." They opened a cage and let a bird go free: "So you'll learn to love the air." They gave him a geranium: "So you'll learn to love the earth." And they gave him a little bottle sealed up tight: "Don't ever, ever open it. So you'll learn to love mystery."[25]

Questions for Reflection

How do you feel about _____ *(name)* being pregnant?

How can we help _____ *(name)* in her pregnancy?

Response

Our response is "Thank you, Living God."

For parents and grandparents. *Response*

For children and all new life. *Response*

For homes and families. *Response*

For water, air, earth and mystery. *Response*

For what else shall we pray? *Pause, then response*

Sending Prayer

Because all of us are called to give birth, we can learn from mothers. May the willingness of women to endure pain and loss fill us with the strength to love and accept the mystery and gift of life.

All extend hands in blessing.

Bless _____ *(name)*. Peace be upon you. Be great with peace. Joy be upon you. Be great with joy. Love be upon you. Be great with love. Mystery be upon you. Be great with mystery. Amen.

*B*lessing for Someone Who Died

Symbol

Cross

Gathering Prayer

We gather in profound sadness, God of Comfort and Consolation.
_____ *(Name)* has died and we come together both to
remember _____ *(name)* and to ask you and our faith family
to be our strength in this painful loss.

Two Candles

In gratitude we pause to remember and name all those who have
died, especially _____ *(name)*.

Pause.

Our lives have been brightened with their love and friendship.
May their goodness and kindness always be remembered.

Light one candle. Be silent.

We pray that all future generations become warm and enduring
lights to one another.

Light second candle. Be silent.

In the present, full of comforting memories and gentle hope, we
ask you, O God, to be our quiet strength and consolation.

Pause.

Reading

Saint John Chrysostom once wrote these consoling words:

> She whom we love and lose is no longer where she was before. She is now wherever we are.[26]

Questions for Reflection

What is your best memory of the person who died?

How can this memory make you a better person?

Response

Our response is "We thank you, Gentle God."

Comforting God, we remember the death of _____ *(name)* whose life touched ours.

Let us feel the presence of _____ *(name)* beside us now.

For all we shared together with _____ *(name)*. *Response*

For life with all its joys and trials. *Response*

For affection and trust. *Response*

For courage to embrace mystery. *Response*

For what else shall we pray? *Pause, then response*

Sending Prayer

Let us carry our good and treasured memories of _____ *(name)* to all those we meet. While we delight in recalling good times, we also express sadness for missed opportunities to show our love and care. May the fruits of our friendship and love be a blessing to all. Amen.

Pass cross. Ask each person to hold it for a moment and image the person who has died and to speak of the loss.

*ℬ*lessing for Death of a Pet

Symbol

Water bowl

Gathering Prayer

Creator of the Universe, all life is holy. In gratitude we gather to remember your gifts of nature and all animal life.

Two Candles

We light a candle of gratitude to our pet, _____ *(name)*. He/she filled us with smiles, gentleness and affection.

Light one candle. Be silent.

We light a second candle to the future and all those who will delight in having pets as companions on their life journeys.

Light second candle. Be silent.

And in the present we ask you, Creator God, to heal us of our heavy hearts as we face the loss of our pet, _____ *(name)*. Make us kind in our relationships with all your creatures and all creation.

Pause.

Reading

Poet Kahlil Gibran once wrote:

> If you would indeed behold the spirit of death, open your heart wide unto the body of life. For life and death are one, even as the river and the sea are one.[27]

Questions for Reflection

What did you like best about _____ *(pet's name)*?

What can we learn from caring for animals?

Response

Our response is "We thank you, God of All Creatures."

For all creation. *Response*

For all life. *Response*

For all animals, fish, dogs, cats, hamsters and birds. *Response*

For our pet, _____ *(name)*. *Response*

As we recall the loyalty of _____ *(name)*, let us remember and share the times when _____. *Pause, then response*

Sending Prayer

Fill us, O God, with new strength in our loss and bless us with hope and a deep love for all the gifts of creation. Amen.

Sprinkle water from bowl on the earth.

ℬlessing for Family Forgiveness

Symbol

Paper and pencil

Gathering Prayer

God of Forgiveness, we need your light to name our wrongs and to ask pardon for what we have done or failed to do.

Two Candles

We kindle a candle to the past. Give us light to see what we have hidden in darkness when we failed to love.

Light one candle. Be silent.

We light a candle to the future. We ask to be aware of the ways God calls us out of darkness into love.

Light second candle. Be silent.

And in the present we name in our hearts our need for forgiveness.

Pause.

Reading

Listen to the wisdom of this Buddhist prayer:

> When someone is wronged, he must put aside all resentment and say, "my mind shall not be disturbed; no anger shall escape my lips; I will remain kind and friendly, with loving thoughts and no secret spite."[28]

Questions for Reflection

What is the best thing you can do when you are hurt by family?

Write down one or two things for which you seek forgiveness.

Response

Our response is "We are sorry."

For blaming or neglecting others. *Response*

For ignoring or forgetting God or others. *Response*

As parent(s) I/we ask forgiveness of you, our children, for anything I/we have done to hurt you. *Response*

As son(s) and daughter(s), we ask you, our parents, for forgiveness for anything we may have done to hurt you. *Response*

Sending Prayer

We, _____ *(names)*, accept family life.

We promise to be with one another in good and bad times.

We promise to be faithful.

We promise to love and to forgive.

We promise to be patient.

We promise to welcome Jesus as friend into our family life.

We promise to honor one another all the days of our life.

We offer a sign of forgiveness *(a hug, kiss, handshake)*.

*B*lessing for Mending Quarrels

Symbol

Tangled threads

Gathering Prayer

Healing God, give our family strength to let go of destructive anger, hurt, and resentment and help us trust that you are always with us. We place our hands in our laps, palms up.

Let us breathe in and say: Let go.

Pause.

And breathe out and say: Heal us.

Two Candles

For all who have been healed in the past.

Light one candle. Be silent.

For all those who will struggle with family hurt in the future.

Light second candle. Be silent.

And in the present help us speak with one another peacefully and gently so that healing may come to our family.

Pause.

Reading

The Medical Mission Sisters write:

> God our Mother, Living Water, River of Mercy, Source of Life, in whom we live and move and have our being, who quenches our thirst, refreshes our weariness, bathes and

washes and cleanses our wounds, be for us always a fountain of life, and for all the world a river of hope springing up in the midst of the deserts of despair. Honor and blessing, glory and praise to You forever. Amen.[29]

Questions for Reflection

How can we heal when we have hurt one another?

How can we avoid hurting one another in the future?

Response

Our response is "Heal us, Forgiving God."

For our hardness of heart. *Response*

For refusing to offer water to the thirsty and refreshment to the weary. *Response*

For tangling the threads of confusion. *Response*

For our unwillingness to listen to one another. *Response*

For focusing on faults rather than strengths. *Response*

For what else shall we pray? *Pause, then response*

Sending Prayer

Help us, Loving God, to go now to our families, workplaces and faith communities and be strong in our promise to be a healing presence to all we meet. Amen.

Invite all to offer some sign of healing to one another.

*B*lessing for the Less Fortunate

Symbol

Evergreen branch

Gathering Prayer

God of Strength and Hope, there are many among us who have little. We gather to remember them and commit ourselves, not just to charity, but to justice throughout the world. Bless us with the constancy of the evergreen and let us live your faithfulness in bringing strength to others.

Two Candles

For all those who held onto their faith and hope despite suffering.

Light one candle. Be silent.

For all those who continue to live without basic human rights and needs: the hungry, homeless and lost.

Light second candle. Be silent.

For all here gathered, may we always be grateful for what we have and work for those less fortunate.

Pause.

Reading

Listen to the wisdom of the Celts:

> You are a shade in the heat. You are a shelter in the cold. You are eyes to the blind. You are a staff to the pilgrim.

You are an island to the sun. You are a stronghold upon land. You are a well in the wasteland. You are healing to the sick.[30]

Questions for Reflection

What is one way you can be a companion to someone in need?

When has someone helped you when you needed something?

Response

Our response is "Help us do justice, Living God."

When we see the hungry, the lonely, the needy. *Response*

May we be a shade and a shelter. *Response*

May we be a staff and stronghold. *Response*

When we feel oppressed ourselves. *Response*

When we hear the poor ridiculed or disparaged. *Response*

For what else shall we pray? *Pause, then response*

Sending Prayer

We are your hands, feet and voice, God of Strength and Hope. Let us reach out for those in need. May we speak powerfully of their human rights to all. Give us courage in our resolve. Work through us so that all might know your care. We make the Sign of the Cross on our hands, feet and throat. Amen.

Blessings for Special Occasions

Blessing for a Birthday

Symbol

Cake and box of birthday candles

Gathering Prayer

God of Life, we have come to celebrate the passing of another year and to ask you to bless us as we begin again. Let _____ *(name)* know of our faithful love and deep care. Together we shout your praises, God of All Birthdays, for all the world to hear.

All: So be it. So be it. So be it.

Two Candles

In gratitude for each day of our lives and all those who gave us life.

Light one candle. Be silent.

In hope that each tomorrow will be full of life and peace.

Light second candle. Be silent.

For all who gather here, especially _____ *(name)*, may this birthday mark the beginning of new and exciting adventures.

Reading

Meister Eckhart wrote:

> My soul is as young as the day it was created.
> Yes, and much younger!
> In fact, I am younger today than I was yesterday
> and if I am not younger tomorrow than I am today

I would be ashamed of myself.
People who dwell in God dwell in the eternal now.
There, people can never grow old.
There, everything is present and everything is new.[31]

Questions for Reflection

What do you think is the best way to celebrate a birthday?

What was your favorite birthday celebration?

Response

Bless _____ *(name)* with gentleness and peace. Give
_____ *(name)* eyes to see, ears to hear and a heart to love the
beauty and wonder of your created world. May _____ *(name)*
be blessed with good health, happiness and hope. We thank you
for parents who have given _____ *(name)* life, and for life
nurturers: sisters, brothers, grandparents, relatives and friends.

*As each person lights a birthday candle from the candle of the
future, place it on the cake and say:* I wish for you _____.

Sending Prayer

Renewed by this birthday celebration, Gentle God, let us be
your blessing of new life to all we meet today. Amen.

*Ask all to hold hands in a circle around the cake and sing
"Happy Birthday."*

Blessing for an Engagement

Symbol

Dried fruits

Gathering Prayer

Loving God, what a joy it is to gather in celebration of the engagement of _____ *(name)* and _____ *(name)*. Our hearts are full of happiness for them as they enter this new phase of their lives. May their love grow and their preparations for marriage be gentle.

Two Candles

In gratitude for those people whose witness of love convinced us that marriage was a wonderful gift.

Light one candle. Be silent.

May the children of tomorrow know the joy of meeting a life partner.

Light second candle. Be silent.

For _____ *(name)* and _____ *(name)*, may their engagement be a time of growth in God's love and love for each other.

Pause.

Reading

Listen to the wisdom of Rumi:

> May these vows and this marriage be blessed.
> May it be sweet milk,
> this marriage, like wine and halvah.

May this marriage offer fruit and shade
like the date palm.
May this marriage be full of laughter,
our every day a day in paradise.
May this marriage be a sign of compassion,
a seal of happiness here and hereafter.
May this marriage have a fair face and a good name,
an omen, as welcome
as the moon in a clear blue sky.
I am out of words to describe
how spirit mingles in this marriage.[32]

Questions for Reflection

What do you wish for the newly engaged couple?

How can we support couples preparing for marriage?

Response

Our response is "Spirit, mingle in our lives."

For _____ *(name)* and _____ *(name)* and all the engaged.
Response

For all seeking new paths. *Response*

For laughter, compassion and happiness. *Response*

For what else shall we pray? *Pause, then response*

Sending Prayer

Watch over _____ *(name)* and _____ *(name)* as they enter
their engagement, God of Enduring Love. And let their love
and care for one another be a constant sign of your love for all.
Amen.

Pass the fruit and invite all to eat.

*B*lessing for a Wedding Anniversary

Symbol

Wedding rings

Gathering Prayer

God of Time and Memories, we come together today to celebrate the strength and love of our friends, _____ *(name and name)* who have been together for _____ *(number of years)*. Thank you for letting them walk with us. May our prayer today strengthen them in their commitment and fidelity. Blessed be the feast of married life.

Two Candles

For all who have been faithful to marriage and life.

Light one candle. Be silent.

For all who will marry in the future.

Light second candle. Be silent.

For _____ *(name and name)* who today celebrate their anniversary.

Pause.

Reading

Saint Catherine of Siena writes:

> I (God) ask you to love me with the same love with which I love you. But for me you cannot do this, for I loved you without being loved. This is why I have put you among your neighbors: so that you can do for them what

you cannot do for me: that is, love them without any concern for thanks and without looking for any profit for yourself. And whatever you do for them I will consider done for me.[33]

Questions for Reflection

What do you value most about marriage?

What do you enjoy most about the married couple celebrating today?

Response

Our response is "Strengthen us, O God."

In all our relationships. *Response*

In the hands we hold in our families. *Response*

In giving thanks for the lighthearted times of laughter, affection, success and happiness. *Response*

In accepting the dark times of misunderstanding, sorrow, injuries and struggles. *Response*

For what else shall we pray? *Pause, then response*

Sending Prayer

Fill us with the strength of this marriage, O God of Holy Love, and let us never be afraid to laugh, cry and trust one another with our deepest feelings and fears. Like these rings, continue to encircle us with your love. Amen.

Extend hands in blessing and say:

Bless this marriage. Bless these lives. Bless these hearts. We love you.

Blessing for Honors and Awards

Symbol

Award

Gathering Prayer

How grateful we are, Majestic God, to share the gifts you so readily offer us. Now as we gather to honor _____ *(name)* who has been recognized for his/her gifts, we praise and thank you.

Two Candles

For all who taught us to accomplish good and have grateful hearts.

Light one candle. Be silent.

May our children welcome honors with humility and thankfulness.

Light second candle. Be silent.

May we together delight in our good fortune.

Pause.

Reading

Molly Fumia wrote:

> Oh Great Spirit of Surprise, dazzle us with a day of amazing embraces, great hearts, and doers of good deeds.[34]

Questions for Reflection

What is the best part of receiving an award or honor?

How can we share honors with others?

Response

Our response is "Fill us with gratitude, Gracious God."

For humility. *Response*

For all your gifts of creation and grace. *Response*

For our families and all the support they offer us. *Response*

For all those who walk quietly with us daily. *Response*

For this honor of _____ *(name)*. *Response*

For what else shall we pray? *Pause, then response*

Sending Prayer

Help us never to be full of ourselves, Humble God. Scripture tells us that Jesus clung to nothing, not even his relationship with you. Show us the path of gratitude and teach us never to take friends, colleagues and family for granted. Amen.

Place your hand on the shoulder of the person being recognized and say:

_____ *(Name)*, thank you for living your gifts for others.

Blessing for a Graduation

Symbol

Diploma

Gathering Prayer

What a wonderful time it is, God of All Our Accomplishments. Today we gather to shout your praises and sing our joy that _____ *(name)* is graduating. Be with us as we pray.

Two Candles

For all those whose witness and encouragement helped us value learning and schooling.

Light one candle. Be silent.

May our children and our children's children have the opportunity for a quality education.

Light second candle. Be silent.

May all of us here rejoice again in each other's gifts and accomplishments.

Pause.

Reading

United Nations secretary-general Dag Hammarskjöld wrote:

> Do not look back. And do not dream about the future, either. It will neither give you back the past, nor satisfy your other daydreams. Your duty, your reward—your destiny—are here and now.[35]

Questions for Reflection

What do you wish for the graduate(s)?

How can we help those graduating to find the next path in their lives?

Response

You are an alleluia, _____ *(name)*, a special, unique, unrepeatable being. There has never been anyone like you and never will be. In all the millions of universes, you were made for this time and this place. If you were not, the world would be different. We would be different. You are the joy of God's creation, _____ *(name)*. We come to reflect on who you are and to celebrate your accomplishments. We bless you in your dreams. We thank you for your gifts of _____, and for living them with us. We love you.

Sending Prayer

Joy is contagious. Teach us to delight in life, Joyful God, and send us as signs of gladness. May all who meet us, meet you.

Let us breathe in: love.

Pause.

And breathe out: joy.

Pause.

Amen.

*B*lessing When Starting a New Job

Symbol

Paycheck

Gathering Prayer

Creator God, work is a human right and a great blessing that enhances our dignity and fosters our hope. In our work, we do more than make a living, we craft our lives. As _____ *(name)* begins a new job, gather us in prayer, encouragement and joy.

Two Candles

For all those whose work-filled lives helped us value having a job that could support us.

Light one candle. Be silent.

For all those who will be anxious about not working and who will seek work in the future.

Light second candle. Be silent.

Strengthened by all who work, we thank God for _____ *(name)* and for the work we have and jobs we do.

Pause.

Reading

Listen to the wisdom of the *Catechism of the Catholic Church:*

> Everyone should be able to draw from work the means of providing for his life and that of his family, and of serving the human community.... [Therefore] access to employment and to professions must be open to all

without unjust discrimination: men and women, healthy and disabled, natives and immigrants.[36]

Questions for Reflection

Ask the person starting a new job: What are your concerns? How does he or she want us to help?

Response

Our response is "We thank you, Living God."

For all of creation. *Response*

For those seeking work. *Response*

For those with new work. *Response*

For all who provide the key to finding work for others. *Response*

For _____ *(name)*, may his/her work be fruitful. *Pause, then response*

Sending Prayer

We leave this place, Creator God, with the hope that we will always be able to find work and the commitment to help those in need of work. We praise you for our work and for your work of creation. Bless us today and always. Amen.

Extend hand to bless workers everywhere. Place hand on head of person entering new job.

*B*lessing for a Promotion

Symbol

Bowl of water and evergreen branch

Gathering Prayer

Generous God, promotions don't come easily or independently. We need others to help us grow and succeed. Help us, God, to be aware of all those who have helped _____ *(name)* to prosper.

Two Candles

In gratitude for all those who convinced us that we had talent and always encouraged us.

Light one candle. Be silent.

May our children always be surrounded by people who support and love them.

Light second candle. Be silent.

May all of us commit ourselves to hard work, growth and the sharing of our talents with the poor.

Pause.

Reading

Listen to the wisdom of this old Gaelic blessing:

> Deep peace of the running wave to you.
> Deep peace of the flowing air to you.
> Deep peace of the quiet earth to you.
> Deep peace of the shining stars to you.

Deep peace of the watching shepherds to you.
Deep peace of the Son of Peace to you.[37]

Questions for Reflection

What do you wish for the person who has been promoted?

How do we thank God when we are honored?

Response

Our response is "Thank you, Loving God."

For honest work and a living wage. *Response*

For all those who help us succeed. *Response*

That we might find ways to help others. *Response*

For this promotion. *Response*

For what else shall we pray? *Pause, then response*

Sending Prayer

Today, O God, we are full of gratitude for all you have given us, especially _____. Help us never forget your bounty and let us be anxious to share it with those most in need. Amen.

Bless the honoree with water, the gift of life for all.

*B*lessing for Retirement

Symbol

Watch

Gathering Prayer

We gather, Holy and Boundless God, to thank you for all
_____ *(name)* has done. May our prayer help her/him find the
transition into retirement a time to relax and do the things
he/she has always dreamed about. Listen to us.

Two Candles

May this light of the past stir up memories of the
accomplishments and contributions _____ *(name)* has
offered to our community and family.

Light one candle. Be silent.

May this candle of the future bring light to new opportunities,
new directions and insights for this next phase of life.

Light second candle. Be silent.

In the present, we remember stories, funny and serious, of who
_____ *(name)* has been for so many people.

Pause.

Reading

Saint Teresa of Avila says:

> Let nothing disturb you,
> nothing cause you fear:

All things pass
God is unchanging.
Patience obtains all:
Whoever has God
Needs nothing else,
God alone suffices.[38]

Questions for Reflection

What do you wish for the person(s) retiring?

How would you like to spend your time when you no longer have to work?

Response

Our response is "Amen."

Show us the path to life, Timeless God. *Response*

Walk with beauty before you. *Response*

Walk with beauty beneath you. *Response*

Walk with beauty behind you. *Response*

Walk with beauty above you. *Response*

Walk with beauty all around you. *Response*

Sending Prayer

Empowered again by your strong love, O God of Gentle Care, we take this gift of retirement to walk in your name to live and be good news to others. We ask that _____ *(name)*'s retirement be a time to know your deep love and care. Amen.

Pass watch and ask each person to make a wish for the person retiring.

Blessing for a New Baby

Symbol

Receiving blanket

Gathering Prayer

How great you are, Gracious God, to give our family and community a new child. How can we thank you enough! Gather us in faith, prayer and enduring gratitude.

Two Candles

For all who have been lights to us: parents, grandparents, teachers and mentors.

Light one candle. Be silent.

For pregnant women and their children and all who will soon be born.

Light second candle. Be silent.

For all gathered here, may we strengthen one another in faith and love.

Pause.

Reading

Listen to the wisdom of the Gospel of Saint Luke:

> People were bringing even infants to him that he might touch them; and when the disciples saw it, they sternly ordered them not to do it. But Jesus called for them and said, "Let the little children come to me, and do not stop them; for it is to such as these that the kingdom of God

belongs. Truly, I tell you, whoever does not receive the kingdom of God as a little child will never enter it." *(18:15-17)*

Questions for Reflection

What does a new child mean to you?

What do you most look forward to with a new baby?

Response

Our response is "Hear us, Gracious God."

For parents everywhere, may they be strong in faith. *Response*

For children, may they always know love. *Response*

For families welcoming new babies, especially _____ *(name)*, may they always be grateful. *Response*

For what else shall we pray? *Pause, then response*

Sending Prayer

You promise, O God, Giver of All Life, that wherever we go, you will be with us. May we never forget your comforting care and may our growing faith be a sign to _____ *(name)* that you will never stop loving us. Amen.

Place receiving blanket on baby and ask each person to make the Sign of the Cross on the baby's forehead.

Blessing for Celebration of the Sacraments

Symbol

Bread

Gathering Prayer

We gather today, Loving and Generous God, to thank you for the gift of sacraments, especially the Sacrament of _____. How fortunate we are to celebrate together the great signs of your love. Help us never to take the power and wonder of the sacraments for granted.

Two Candles

In gratitude we mention all the people who made the celebration of sacraments special times: _____ *(names).*

Light one candle. Be silent.

In the hope that our children will have a deep love for the sacraments.

Light second candle. Be silent.

May _____ *(name)* remember this day of celebrating the Sacrament of _____ and remember our love with special delight.

Pause.

Reading

Theologian and author Joseph Martos writes:

> Sacraments are symbolic ways we tell ourselves and others what we are all about as Christians and as church.

But they are more than signs. They are celebrations of what they signify and so they remind us that the truths and realities that make life worth living are also worth celebrating.[39]

Questions for Reflection

What is your best memory of one of the sacraments?

How can each of us make sacramental celebrations more meaningful?

Response

Our response is "We walk in the newness of life."

For our celebration of the Sacrament of _____ today.
Response

For _____ *(name)*, may we always love one another in faith.
Response

For the people who gathered today, relatives and friends.
Response

For what else shall we pray? *Pause, then response*

Sending Prayer

Gracious and Generous God, thank you for the gift of today. We are so grateful to celebrate and proclaim your sacramental gifts. Let _____ *(name)* walk strongly with this new support for faith and never forget the signs of your love. Amen.

Break bread, pass and eat it.

*B*lessing Before a Journey

Symbol

A compass

Gathering Prayer

Traveling God, you always lead your people home by promising to be our companion on every journey. As you walk with us, open our spirits to amazement and awe and surprise us with the unexpected.

Two Candles

For all those who have traveled with us in faith, we are grateful.

Light one candle. Be silent.

For all those who will travel with us in the future, we are hopeful.

Light second candle. Be silent.

For all those who travel with us now, may God bless our journeys.

Pause.

Reading

Author Gaynell Bordes Cronin writes:

> God of all journeys, you call us to travel the known and unknown paths of life. Protect the way. Lighten our traveling feet. Guide and direct our restless spirits. Answer the needs of our searching hearts. Make safe all the roads of life. And make our journey, your journey, God.[40]

Questions for Reflection

What simple things could we do while we travel to help us stay aware of God?

What is the best trip you have taken?

Response

Our response is "Be with us, O God."

On all our journeys. *Response*

When we are tempted to stray from the right path. *Response*

When we are lost. *Response*

When we forget who we are. *Response*

For what else shall we pray? *Pause, then response*

Sending Prayer

Watch over us as we travel, God of Journeys, and may we breathe your love along the way. Let us warm our hands by the candles of the past and future for courage and strength on our journeys.

Extend hands.

Amen.

Blessings for the Year

*B*lessing for Advent

Symbol

Advent wreath

Gathering Prayer

In this season of Advent, as we gather to wait in the darkness of winter nights for Jesus our Light to come, may our hearts be filled with your joy and promise.

Two Candles

For men and women of long ago who kept alive the promise of Emmanuel, God with us.

Light one candle. Be silent.

For the people of tomorrow, receivers of the promise through us.

Light second candle. Be silent.

In the present, we kindle the light of our Christ candle and see God's promise and presence in the light and dark of our lives.

Light Advent wreath candles.

Pause.

Reading

Poet Jessica Powers proclaims:

> I live my Advent in the womb of Mary.
> And on one night when a great star swings free
> from its high mooring and walks down the sky
> to be the dot above the Christus I,
> I shall be born of her by blessed grace.

I wait in Mary-darkness, faith's walled place,
with hope's expectance of nativity.
I knew for long she carried and fed me,
guarded and loved me, though I could not see.
But only now, with inward jubilee,
I come upon earth's most amazing knowledge:
someone is hidden in this dark with me.[41]

Questions for Reflection

What do you like most about Advent?

How do you prepare for Christmas?

Response

Our response is "In our darkness and in our light."

Carry us and feed us. *Response*

Show us a walking star. *Response*

Secure us in a walled place of faith. *Response*

Be our inward joy and jubilee. *Response*

For what else shall we pray? *Pause, then response*

Sending Prayer

We give thanks for the people in our lives who bring warmth and light to others: _____ *(names)*. We warm our hands by the Advent wreath candles and go forth in the promise.

*B*lessing for Christmas

Symbol

Baby Jesus from nativity scene

Gathering Prayer

As we come together to remember your birth, Newborn God, fill us with the light, hope and the peace that will allow us to transform the world.

Two Candles

For all those who, like the Christ Child, brought new light into our lives.

Light one candle. Be silent.

For all those who will be challenged to be a light in the world of tomorrow.

Light second candle. Be silent.

For all of us on Christmas, may this day give us all new birth.

Pause.

Reading

The prophet Isaiah writes:

> The people who walked in darkness have seen a great light; those who lived in a land of deep darkness—on them light has shined. You have multiplied the nation, you have increased its joy; ...For a child has been born for us, a son given to us; authority rests upon his shoulders; and he is named Wonderful Counselor, Mighty God,

Everlasting Father, Prince of Peace. His authority shall grow continually, and there shall be endless peace.... *(9:2-3a, 6-7a)*

Questions for Reflection

What is most important for you about Christmas?

How do you spread Christmas joy and light to others?

Response

Our response is "A child is born to us, a son is given to us."

For all creation. *Response*

For our families, friends, church and world. *Response*

For those who bring light to darkness. *Response*

For what else shall we pray? *Pause, then response*

Sending Prayer

Each day holds the promise of new birth. Let us offer hope and possibility to all we meet. May all know your love imprinted on their hearts, Caring God, by the way we honor them. Amen.

All toast: Christmas light, a blessed Christmas.

*B*lessing for a New Year

Symbol

Bells

Gathering Prayer

In gathering as family we find in one another the hope and joy of a new beginning, God of All Times. Together, we welcome a new year.

Ring bells.

Two Candles

In this candlelight, we recall one peace-filled gift that has come to us during the past year.

Light one candle. Be silent.

In all our tomorrows, may we be a sign of peace in our world.

Light second candle. Be silent.

In our today, we ask forgiveness of anyone we may have hurt by offering a sign of peace.

Pause.

Reading

The woman known as the Peace Pilgrim writes:

> Every good thing you do,
> every good thing you say,
> every good thought you think,
> vibrates on and on and never

ceases... the good,
remains forever.[42]

Questions for Reflection

What are you looking forward to this new year?

What other ways can we celebrate a new year?

Response

Ring bells. Our response is "Ring out the old, ring in the new."

Ring happy bells across the snow,
The year is going, let it go.
Ring out the false, ring in the true. *Response*

Ring out the feud of rich and poor.
Ring out the want, the hurt, the sad,
The faithless coldness of the times no more. *Response*

Ring out the thousand wars of old,
Ring in the thousand years of peace,
Ring in the love of truth and right. *Response*

Ring in the valiant, true and free,
Ring out the darkness of the land.
Ring in the Christ that is to be. *Response*

For what else shall we ring out the old and ring in the new?

Pause, then response

Sending Prayer

Jesus is the same yesterday, today and forever. We send God's blessing of peace for this year 20__.

Extend hands and turn to bless the four directions and say:

May you live in peace.

Blessing for Epiphany

Symbol

Star

Gathering Prayer

God of All Epiphanies, you show yourself in Jesus to all people on this twelfth night of Christmas. With the Wise Ones of the East we thank you for giving us gifts of stars to follow, journeys to take and surprise adventures.

Two Candles

In gratitude for your protection in all our past comings and goings,

Light one candle. Be silent.

In hope for peace in the future as we greet and welcome strangers and guests.

Light second candle. Be silent.

For the gift of one another: _____ *(name people)*, we thank you.

Pause.

Reading

Abbie Graham writes:

> I open the door. The gorgeous guest from afar sweeps in. In her hands are gifts—the gifts of hours and far-seeing moments, the gift of mornings and evenings, the gift of spring and summer, the gift of autumn and winter. She must have searched the heavens for boons so rare.[43]

Questions for Reflection

How do you see God in your life?

What customs from other cultures would you like to add to the celebration of Epiphany (for example, Hispanic customs)?

Response

Our response is "Make us gifts to others."

In all our foreseeing moments. *Response*

In all our mornings, evenings and seasons. *Response*

In all light and darkness. *Response*

In all journeys and searchings. *Response*

In all doorways of welcoming and sending. *Response*

For what else shall we pray? *Pause, then response*

Sending Prayer

We continue the tradition of blessing homes on the feast of Epiphany and pray:

God of All Homes, we welcome you.

Bless our home with your presence.

Bless our doorways, windows, rooms.

Bless our hearts with your love.

Bless our hopes, dreams and joys.

Bless the spaces of our home.

Make them holy with your Starlight. Amen.

Open the door.

Blessing for Lent

Symbol

Cross

Gathering Prayer

To begin the season of Lent we come together as family before the cross, a sign of our 40-day journey toward Easter. God of Lenten Walks, help us pay attention to you in our life through prayer, penance and doing acts of loving kindness as we take up our cross and follow Jesus.

Two Candles

In the light of the past we see and name our weaknesses and strengths in walking with Jesus.

Light one candle. Be silent.

We whisper to the people of the future not to be afraid of hardships in following Jesus.

Light second candle. Be silent.

This Lent we promise to do one thing to become more aware of God in ourselves and others.

Pause.

Reading

The Book of Joel tells us:

> Yet even now, says the Lord, return to me with all your heart, with fasting, with weeping, and with mourning; rend your hearts and not your clothing. Return to the

Lord, your God, for he is gracious and merciful, slow to anger, and abounding in steadfast love.... *(2:12-13)*

Questions for Reflection

What one thing do you plan to do to make Lent meaningful?

How can you help others live Lent well?

Response

Our response is "Amen."

Come back to God with all your heart. *Response*

Leave the past in ashes. *Response*

Turn to God with prayers and fasting. *Response*

For God is tender and compassionate. *Response*

To what else shall we say Amen? *Pause, and response*

Sending Prayer

Let us go forth to love and serve God through the way we live our Lenten promises. As we make the Sign of the Cross on the forehead of each person, we say: Keep Lent and turn to God with all your heart.

*B*lessing for Easter

Symbol

Easter lily

Gathering Prayer

We thank you, Risen God, for overcoming death and promising us life. As we gather today, let us be a life-giving presence to one another.

Two Candles

For all those whose belief in life helped us overcome death.

Light one candle. Be silent.

For all the children of tomorrow, may they always enjoy a life of faith.

Light second candle. Be silent.

For all gathered here, may we and our homes be filled with Easter joy, peace, laughter and love.

Pause.

Reading

Listen to the Gospel of Saint Matthew:

> [T]he angel said to the women, "Do not be afraid; I know that you are looking for Jesus who was crucified. He is not here; for he has been raised, as he said. Come, see the place where he lay." *(28:5-6)*

Questions for Reflection

How can we bring the message of Easter—life forever—to our daily lives?

How does your favorite Easter tradition reflect the Risen Jesus?

Response

Our response is "We thank you, Risen God."

For all the gifts of creation. *Response*

For our faith which assures us that we will live forever. *Response*

For all gathered here that we might always give life to one another. *Response*

For the scent of these flowers, may they be a sign of joy, hope and the new life of spring which follows the cold and dark of winter. *Response*

For what else shall we pray? *Pause, then response*

Sending Prayer

The promise of everlasting life fills us with hope, newly Risen God. Make us unafraid to proclaim your promises with the passion of our lives and the gentleness of our love. Amen.

All toast: Easter Life, a blessed Easter.

Blessing for Pentecost

Symbol

Feather

Gathering Prayer

Spirit of God, you are present everywhere, pervading our lives like the air we breathe, like the wind that blows, like the life that flows through our being. May we be carried like a feather on the breath of your love to serve others on this feast of Pentecost.

Two Candles

We light a candle to the past to help us see the fears and trembling that hinder and block the Holy Spirit's life in us.

Light one candle. Be silent.

We light a candle to the future to warm the hearts of children everywhere that they may be awake and alert to the Holy Spirit as giver of life and gifts.

Light second candle. Be silent.

In the present, may we together experience the Holy Spirit among us—nearer to us than we are to ourselves.

Pause.

Reading

Hildegard of Bingen writes:

> But I am continuously filled with fear and trembling. For I do not recognize in myself security through any kind of

personal ability. And yet I raise my hands aloft to God, that I might be held by God, just like a feather which has no weight from its own strength and lets itself be carried by the wind.[44]

Questions for Reflection

When have you felt like a feather in God's hand?

How have you seen the Holy Spirit work in others' lives?

Response

Our response is "Come, Spirit, come."

Be wind to bring healing. *Response*

Be breath to bring life. *Response*

Be a flame to bring light and warmth. *Response*

Be water to give drink. *Response*

Be a dove bringing peace. *Response*

For what else shall we ask the Spirit? *Pause, then response*

Sending Prayer

Clothe us with your Spirit. Carry us as a feather on the wind of your love to the north, south, east and west. We remember your promise: I am with you always. And we promise: We are with you always. Amen.

Ask all to breathe in God's spirit and breathe out God's life in all creation.

Blessing for Mother's Day

Symbol

Heart

Gathering Prayer

Where would we be, O God of All Goodness, without our mothers? Today, as we gather to honor the women who gave us life, nourished and nurtured us, let us put aside all our differences as a way to praise them and you.

Two Candles

For all who have died: grandmothers, godmothers, mentors.

Light one candle. Be silent.

For all mothers who will give birth in the future.

Light second. Be silent.

For each of our mothers, may they be filled with pride and hope. We share those qualities we admire in our mothers, or the women who nurtured us: _____ *(names)*.

Pause.

Reading

Belleruth Naparstek writes:

> Just give me this:
> a rinsing out, a cleansing free of all my smaller strivings.
> So I can be...
> True to my purpose,
> All my energy aligned behind my deepest intention...

So I can start over,
Fresh and clean
Like sweet sheets billowing in the summer sun,
My heart pierced with gratitude.[45]

Questions for Reflection

Besides life, what is the most important gift your mother gave you?

How can we bring our mother's best qualities to others?

Response

Our response is "God of Holy People, bless them."

For our grandmothers, mothers and friends. *Response*

For all who care for us like mothers. *Response*

For children without mothers. *Response*

For what else shall we pray? *Pause, then response*

Sending Prayer

Fill us, Gentle God, with the tenderness of mothers who have just given birth. Remind us, wherever we go, that people are always in need of simple touch, an open ear and heart, and the courage to live life fully. Let our mothers live forever in our hearts. Amen.

Sign your heart and then sign the forehead of your mother or another woman of influence in your life and say:

I love you. I am so glad you are in my life.

*B*lessing for Father's Day

Symbol

Cap

Gathering Prayer

We come together today, dear God, to honor our fathers, our dads, our pops, our friends and teachers. Let them feel the power of our love surrounding them and may they be strengthened to continue to give to all those in need.

Two Candles

For all, who like fathers, guided us in the past.

Light one candle. Be silent.

For all called to fatherhood in the future.

Light second candle. Be silent.

For our fathers, who give us care and protection, love and direction, may they always know we love them. We share those qualities we admire in our fathers or guardians: _____.

Pause.

Reading

Listen to the wisdom of the Book of Sirach:

> Honor your father by word and deed, that his blessing may come upon you. For a father's blessing strengthens the houses of the children...My child, help your father in his old age, and do not grieve him as long as he lives;

even if his mind fails, be patient with him... For kindness to a father will not be forgotten... *(3:8-9,12-14)*

Questions for Reflection

What are you most grateful for from your father?

How can we be like a father to those most in need?

Response

Our response is "Blessed are you God, Father of All Life."

May we care for all creation. *Response*

May we honor our fathers by word and deed. *Response*

May we be like fathers to all in need. *Response*

May we have the courage to be humble. *Response*

For what else shall we pray? *Pause, then response*

Sending Prayer

God, as we continue our life journeys, make us deeply conscious that you are always with us as Guide, Companion, Friend and Father. And let us live as your children wherever we go. Amen.

Place cap on Dad's head. Give him a hug and say: Be dressed by our love for you.

Blessing for Independence Day

Symbol

U.S. flag

Gathering Prayer

Thank you, O God, for the freedom we have to speak, to listen, to worship and to gather in faith in our country. Today, as we celebrate our nation's birthday, let us be especially mindful of the rights we enjoy and our obligation to be peacemakers.

Two Candles

For all those in our country who gave their lives to preserve our liberty and promote peace rooted in justice.

Light one candle. Be silent.

For all those who will be challenged to find new and nonviolent ways of resolving differences.

Light second candle. Be silent.

May all here today rejoice in the light of freedom and faith.

Pause.

Reading

The Declaration of Independence reads:

> We hold these Truths to be self-evident, that all men are created equal, that they are endowed by their Creator with certain unalienable rights, that among these are Life, Liberty, and the Pursuit of Happiness.

Questions for Reflection

What do you value most about the United States?

How can you spread the message of equality for all?

Response

Our response is "We are not free until all people are free."

Everyone has the right to freedom of thought, of conscience, of religion. *Response*

Everyone has the right to freedom of opinion and expression. *Response*

Everyone has the right to take part in the government of his or her country. *Response*

Everyone has the right to work. *Response*

Everyone has the right to rest and leisure. *Response*

Everyone has the right to a standard of living adequate to the needs of the person and family.[46] *Response*

Sending Prayer

We are your servants, O God of Life and Liberty. Send us as protectors of human rights, voices of the poor and friends of our enemies. Amen.

Wave the flag of freedom.

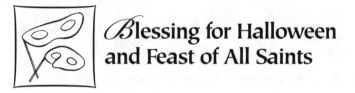

ℬlessing for Halloween and Feast of All Saints

Symbol

Masks

Gathering Prayer

We gather, Joyful God, to remember all those powerful women and men of faith who lived gospel lives. Be with us as individuals and as a family and help us remember that we, too, are called to be saints.

Two Candles

May the light of gospel men and women remind us that God is always with us no matter how far we wander away.

Light one candle. Be silent.

May the light of future saints, with all its possibilities, beckon us to begin again.

Light second candle. Be silent.

And in the present, may we take God's steady arm as we try to become holy men and women today.

Pause.

Reading

In the Book of Revelation we read:

> There was a great multitude that no one could count, from every nation, from all tribes and peoples and languages, standing before the throne and before the Lamb, robed in white, with palm branches in their hands…. Then one of

the elders [asked]: "Who are these, robed in white, and where do they come from?" Then he said to me, "These are they who have come out of the great ordeal...."
(7:9, 13-14)

Questions for Reflection

What does it mean to be a saint or to be holy?

What saint or holy person do you most admire?

Response

Our response is "Help us live holy lives."

In all our struggles. *Response*

In all our joys. *Response*

For the saints after whom we are named. *Response*

As an example for those seeking the gospel. *Response*

For what else shall we pray? *Pause, then response*

Sending Prayer

Let the costumes we wear this Halloween, O God, remind us of all that you would have us be. And as we celebrate the feast of All Saints, let us never wear a mask to hide from you or one another. We ask you to hear us through all the saints who have gone before us and all those who will follow us. Amen.

Ask all to bless themselves with the Sign of the Cross.

Blessing for Thanksgiving

Symbol

Blessing cup

Gathering Prayer

How thankful we are, Gracious God, for all you do for us. Today as we gather to celebrate with family and friends, help us never to take for granted all our gifts, particularly the gift of one another.

Two Candles

For families everywhere who have gathered to celebrate Thanksgiving in the past.

Light one candle. Be silent.

For all those who will gather in gratitude in the future.

Light second candle. Be silent.

Today, we thank you for the people around this table. We name those whom we love and are not present: _____ *(names).*

Pause.

We hold hands and share our individual prayers of thanksgiving:

Reading

Listen to the wisdom of Saint John Chrysostom:

> God gave us one house for all to dwell in. It is called the world. God distributed all things equally. He kindled one sun for all: stretched above us one roof, one sky, and set

our table which is the earth. And God gave us another table of one loaf and one cup.[47]

Questions for Reflection

For what are you most thankful this year?

What Thanksgiving was especially meaningful to you?

Response

Our response is "We give you thanks, O God."

God, Giver of Gifts, we thank you for calling us to be your family. As we lift this blessing cup to you in gratitude, we praise you for your many favors and thank you for those present at our table: *(Name all present).*

For the bountiful gifts of creation. *Response*

For all nations and cultures. *Response*

For our family, friends, church and nation. *Response*

For the one house, one roof, one sky, one table, one loaf, one cup. *Response*

Sending Prayer

Watch over us each day, Loving God, and make us conscious of your never-ending care for us. Let the gratitude we know today seep like a gentle rain into the lives and hearts of all people we meet in your world and at your table. Amen.

Pass and drink from the cup of blessing.

*&*ndnotes

1 The Maryknoll Sisters Calendar for 2000, Teresa of Avila.

2 Kent Nerburn, *Letters to My Son* (Novato, Calif.: New World Library, 1999), as found in *Spiritual Literacy: Reading the Sacred in Everyday Life,* by Frederic Brussat, Mary Ann Brussat (New York: Scribner, 1996), p. 259.

3 T. S. Eliot, "The Rock," *Collected Poems* (Orlando, Fla.: Harcourt Brace Jovanovich, 1963).

4 Megan McKenna, *Parables: The Arrows of God* (Maryknoll, N.Y.: Orbis Books, 1994), as found in *Spiritual Literacy,* p. 490.

5 *The New American Bible With Revised New Testament* (Washington, D.C.: Confraternity of Christian Doctrine, 1991).

6 Julian of Norwich, *Showings,* trans. Edmund Colledge and James Walsh (New York: Paulist Press, 1978), p. 183.

7 *Life Prayers,* p. 112.

8 Yajur Veda, in *World Scripture,* Andrew Wilson, ed. (New York: International Religious Foundation, 1995), 36.18, p. 161.

9 *Peace,* a Reflection Film, used with permission of Ikonographics, 1976.

10 *As Above, So Below,* ed. Ronald Miller and the Editors of the New Age Journal (New York: J. P. Tarcher, 1992), p. 28.

11 The Prophet Muhammad in *Life Prayers: From Around the World: 365 Prayers, Blessings, and Affirmations to Celebrate the Human Journey,* edited by Elizabeth J. Roberts and Elias Amidon (San Francisco: HarperSanFrancisco, 1996), p. 109.

12 Henry Miller, *As Above, So Below,* p. 36.

13 Margaret Dorgan, quoting Thérèse of Lisieux in *Thérèse of Lisieux, Mystic of the Ordinary,* Spiritual Life 35:4.

14 Nelson Mandela in *Life Prayers,* p. 127.

15 *Catherine of Siena: The Dialogue,* trans. and introduction of Suzanne Noffke, O.P. (New York: Paulist Press, 1980), p. 360.

16 Brian Cavanaugh, T.O.R., *The Sower's Seeds* (Mahwah, N.J.: Paulist Press, 1990).

17 Jacob Needleman, *Money and the Meaning of Life* (New York: Doubleday, 1991), as quoted in *Spiritual Literacy,* p. 314.

18 Wu-Men, *Life Prayers,* p. 301.

19 "An American Indian Prayer," from War Resisters League, New York, *Peace Calendar,* As Long as the Rivers Flow, 1974.

20 Hinduism, Garuda Purana 115, *World Scripture,* p. 564.

21 Noela Evans, *Meditations for the Passages and Celebrations of Life* (New York: Harmony Books, 1994), as quoted in: *Spiritual Literacy,* p. 99.

22 Sidney Lovett, *Courage to Change: One Day at a Time In Alanon II* (New York: Al-Anon Family Group Headquarters, 1992).

23 Rabbi Rami Shapiro, *A Plea for Healing,* in *Life Prayers,* p. 269.

24 Robert Johnson in *We: Understanding the Psychology of Romantic Love* (New York: Harper Collins, 1983), as quoted in *Spiritual Literacy,* pp. 441-2.

25 Eduardo Galeano, *Walking Words,* trans. Mark Fried (New York: W. W. Norton and Company, Inc.), in *Spiritual Literacy,* pp. 50-51.

26 Saint John Chrysostom in *Life Prayers,* p. 341.

27 Kahlil Gibran, *The Prophet* (New York: Alfred Knopf, 1951), in *Life Prayers,* p. 331.

28 *The Garden Treasury of Prayers for Boys and Girls* (Racine, Wisc.: Western Publishing Co. Inc., 1975), p. 16.

29 Miriam Therese Winter, *Woman Prayer, Woman Song* (Oak Park, Ill.: Meyer Stone Books, 1987, in *Life Prayers,* p. 279.

30 Kent Nerburn, "Letters to My Son" (Novato, Calif.: New World Library, 1999), in *Spiritual Literacy,* p. 259.

31 *Meditations With Meister Eckhart,* trans. Matthew Fox (Santa Fe, NM: Bear and Company, 1983), p. 32.

32 Jalal Al-Din Rumi, *Love Is a Stranger* (Putney, Vt.: Threshold Books, 1993), *Life Prayers,* p. 239.

33 Patricia Mary Vinje, *Praying with Catherine of Siena* (Winona, Minn.: St. Mary's Press, 1990), p. 42.

34 *Prayers for Healing: 365 Blessings, Poems, and Meditations From Around the World,* ed. Maggie Oman and Larry Dossey (Berkeley, Calif.: Conari Press, 1997), p. 51.

35 Dag Hammarskjöld, *Markings* (New York: Knopf, 1969), p. 174.

36 *Catechism of the Catholic Church* (Washington, D.C.: United States Catholic Conference, 1994), #2428 and #2433.

37 *Pocketful of Miracles,* ed. Joan Borysendo, Ph.D. (New York: Warner Books, 1994), p. 404.

38 Teresa of Avila, *Saints for All Seasons,* ed. John J. Delaney (Garden City, N.Y.: Doubleday and Co., 1978), p. 128.

39 Joseph Martos, "Liturgy and Life: Sacraments, Celebration of our Faith and Life," *The Catechist,* October, 1993, p. 52.

40 Gaynell Cronin, "Blessing for Travel," *Best of Holydays and Holidays* (Cincinnati, Ohio: St. Anthony Messenger Press), p. 98.

41 Jessica Powers, *Selected Poetry,* ed. Regina Siegfried, A.S.C., and Robert Morneau (Kansas City, Mo.: Sheed and Ward, 1989), p. 81.

42 *Pocketful of Miracles,* p. 400.

43   Abbie Graham, as quoted in *Simple Abundance: A Daybook of Comfort and Joy* (New York: Warner Books, 1995).

44   *Book of Divine Works,* ed. Matthew Fox (Sante Fe, N.M.: Bear & Co., 1987), p. 347.

45   Belleruth Naparstek, *Prayers for Healing,* ed. Maggie Oman (Berkeley, Calif.: Conari Press, 1997), p. 188.

46   Adapted from the Declaration of Human Rights of the United Nations, December 10, 1948.

47   Saint John Chrysostom, as told by Gaynell Cronin in *Sunday Throughout the Week* (Notre Dame, Ind.: Ave Maria Press, 1981), p. 105.